GRADES 4–8

Text-Marking Lessons
for Active Nonfiction Reading

Reproducible Nonfiction Passages With Lessons That Guide Students to
Read Strategically, Identify Text Structures, and Activate Comprehension

Judith Bauer Stamper

New York • Toronto • London • Auckland • Sydney **Teaching**
Mexico City • New Delhi • Hong Kong • Buenos Aires *Resources*

Editor: Mela Ottaiano

Cover design: Brian LaRossa

Interior design: Melinda Belter

Interior illustrations and photos: page 16: ktsdesign/Bigstock.com; page 17: SecureSpace/Bigstock.com; page 20: © AP Images; page 21: DK1vision/Bigstock.com; page 24: gtrmtt84/Bigstock.com; page 25: 1photo/Bigstock.com; page 28: anatomyofrockthe/Bigstock.com; page 29: nekitt/Bigstock.com; page 32: kotse/Bigstock.com; page 36: Gudella/Bigstock.com; page 37: desertrosestudios/Bigstock.com; page 40: JeanneD/Bigstock.com; page 41: mjpixel/Bigstock.com; page 44: DmitryP/Bigstock.com; page 45: cozyta/Bigstock.com; page 48: jaboardm/Bigstock.com; page 52: mikess5/Bigstock.com; page 56: tom oliveira/Bigstock.com; page 57: JamesBustraan/Bigstock.com

ISBN: 978-0-545-28819-4

Copyright © 2012 by Judith Bauer Stamper
All rights reserved. Published by Scholastic Inc.
Printed in the U.S.A.

2 3 4 5 6 7 8 9 10   40   18 17 16 15 14 13 12

Contents

Introduction **5**

Connections to the Common Core State Standards 5

How to Use the CD With the Interactive Whiteboard 6

How to Use the Lessons 6

Teaching Routine 8

Assessment 9

Lesson 1: Read for Details • State Names **10**

Reading 1: Fifty Nifty Names 11

Reading 2: Native Names 12

Reading 3: Kings and Colors 13

Lesson 2: Main Idea & Details • Insect Attacks **14**

Reading 1: Buzz and Bite 15

Reading 2: That Stings! 16

Reading 3: Bad Bug Bites 17

Lesson 3: Sequence of Events • Extreme Survivors **18**

Reading 1: Tsunami Survivor 19

Reading 2: Air Crash Survivor 20

Reading 3: Earthquake Survivor 21

Lesson 4: Summarize • Amazon Rain Forest. **22**

Reading 1: The Amazing Amazon 23

Reading 2: Amazon Journey 24

Reading 3: A Rain Forest in Trouble 25

Lesson 5: Cause & Effect • Volcanoes **26**

Reading 1: Mount St. Helens Blows Up! 27

Reading 2: When Volcanoes Explode 28

Reading 3: Ash From Iceland 29

Lesson 6: Draw Conclusions • Sports Stars **30**

   Reading 1: Wilma Rudolph 31

   Reading 2: Bruce Lee 32

   Reading 3: Pele 33

Lesson 7: Problem & Solution • Rescue Teams **34**

   Reading 1: Buried Alive! 35

   Reading 2: Air Lifts 36

   Reading 3: Animal Emergencies 37

Lesson 8: Compare & Contrast • Predator Power **38**

   Reading 1: Komodo Dragons 39

   Reading 2: Vampire Bats 40

   Reading 3: Great White Sharks 41

Lesson 9: Make Inferences • Record Breakers **42**

   Reading 1: Champion Skippers 43

   Reading 2: Youngest Climber 44

   Reading 3: Wheelchair Champ 45

Lesson 10: Fact & Opinion • Up for Debate **46**

   Reading 1: Should Students Go to School Year-Round? 47

   Reading 2: Should Girls Play on Boys' Sports Teams? 48

   Reading 3: Should Cell Phones Be Allowed in School? 49

Lesson 11: Context Clues • Good as Gold **50**

   Reading 1: A Precious Metal 51

   Reading 2: Hidden Treasure 52

   Reading 3: Panning for Gold 53

Lesson 12: Author's Purpose • Natural Wonders **54**

   Reading 1: The Grandest Canyon 55

   Reading 2: Wild Water Rafting/My Mule Pokey 56

   Reading 3: Grassy Waters/Everglades Adventure 57

Answer Key **58**

Lesson-by-Lesson Connections to the Common Core State Standards . . **64**

Introduction

Students at all grade levels must use reading comprehension skills in every class, every day. Therefore, the ability to comprehend text is an essential ingredient for academic success. To help student achieve their academic goals, introduce them to text marking—a proven, powerful tool for building comprehension skills.

Text-Marking Lessons for Active Nonfiction Reading provides engaging, ready-to-use readings for 12 key comprehension skills. The readings are organized around high-interest topics connected to the curriculum. They are specially written to engage students' interest and specially formatted to provide practice with text marking. When enhanced with an interactive whiteboard, the readings allow students to "get into" and comprehend text in new and rewarding ways.

Why is text marking such an effective tool for comprehension? Marking a text focuses students' attention by giving them concrete tasks. Circling a cause, underlining its effect, and boxing the signal word puts students inside the text. They become involved in active reading as they mark key comprehension elements. Text marking also helps students make the cognitive transfer between the text and comprehension. In addition, it high-lights the importance of justifying an answer with evidence from the text.

For teachers, text marking provides quick and concrete evidence of whether or not students are on task and an accurate snapshot of skills students have mastered and skills they need to work on. Assessment is both concrete and constructive. The lessons in *Text-Marking Lessons for Active Nonfiction Reading* provide readings for teaching and modeling a skill, practicing a skill, and applying the skill. The gradual release instructional model is easy to follow and provides best practices for comprehension learning.

Text marking gives you an effective way to help students interact with text and improve their reading comprehension.

Connections to the Common Core State Standards

The Common Core State Standards emphasize the importance of close attention to the text and its features. Text marking provides an extremely effective tool to focus students on the dimensions of text complexity. For example, the lessons guide students to analyze meaning and purpose by making inferences and identifying author's purpose. Students focus on text structure by text marking sequence of events, cause and effect, and problem and solution. Most important, text marking helps students identify evidence in the text to support their comprehension.

All 12 lessons in this book meet the following College and Career Readiness Anchor Standards for Reading:

R.CCR.1: Read closely to determine what the text says explicitly and to make logical inferences from it; cite specific textual evidence when writing or speaking to support conclusions drawn from the text.

R.CCR.4: Interpret words and phrases as they are used in a text.

For a breakdown of how each lesson connects to the Common Core State Standards for English Language Arts, refer to the chart on page 64. Please visit www.corestandards.org for more details about the standards.

How to Use the CD With the Interactive Whiteboard

The CD includes 12 PDF files—one for each lesson—that contain all of the passages from the printed book. As soon as possible, transfer these files to the computer connected to your interactive whiteboard. Once they are in your computer, you can then import them into the whiteboard software for interactive use with your students. Taking care of this step in advance saves valuable class time and also helps when you want to save edited samples for future reference.

If you are using SMART Notebook™ software for the SMART Board® or any other interactive whiteboard software, be sure you have installed the latest version. (This product was tested using the following software: Notebook for the SMART Board, version 10.7.154.0, and ActiveInspire software for the Promethean ActivBoard, version 1.5.37817.)

How to Use the Lessons

Each lesson consists of four pages of instruction, readings, and text-marking activities.

The **Teaching Plan** gives you specific instructions and tips for teaching each skill through a set of three readings.

Prompts for engaging prior knowledge

Definitions for introducing the skill

Language for modeling the skill

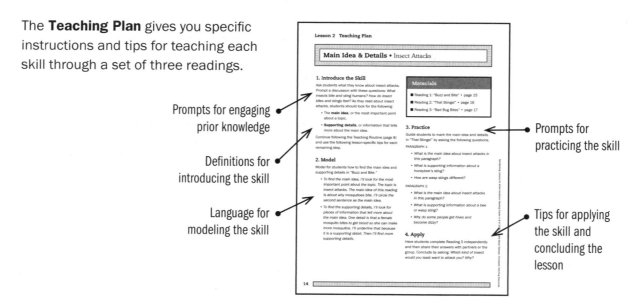

Prompts for practicing the skill

Tips for applying the skill and concluding the lesson

Reading 1 introduces the topic for the lesson and provides a passage for you to model the comprehension skill.

Passage to model the comprehension strategy

Text marks for identifying the skill

Definitions for reinforcing the skill

Directions for marking the text

Reading 2 provides a longer text for you to use with students to practice the skill together. It elaborates on the lesson topic.

Passage to practice the comprehension strategy

Directions for marking the text

Reading 3 provides another text for students to use independently to apply the skill. It extends the lesson topic.

Passage to apply the comprehension strategy

Directions for marking the text

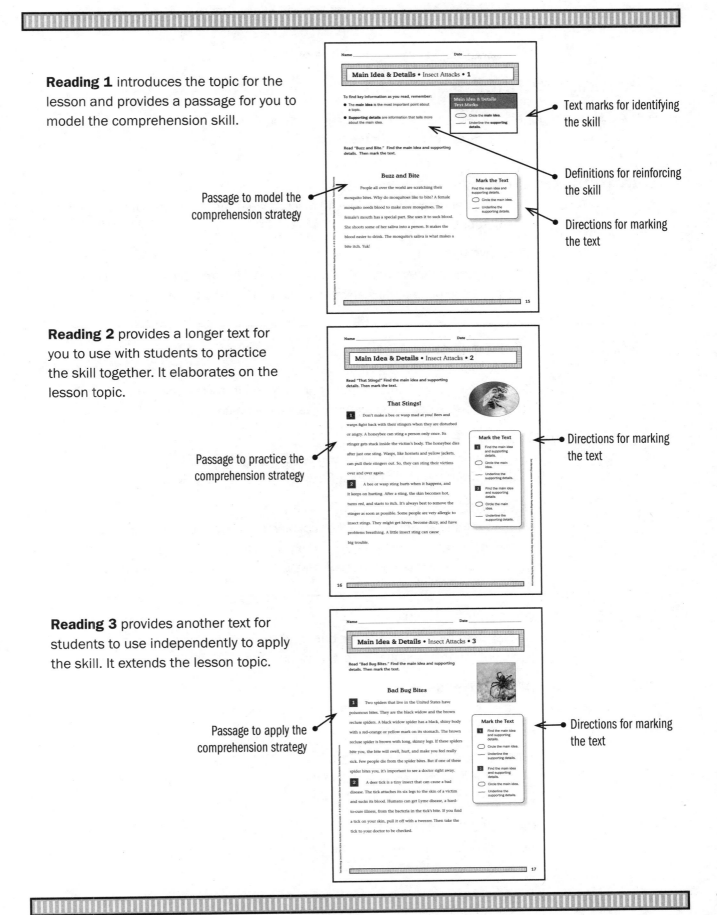

Teaching Routine

Follow this routine for each lesson, using the specific instructional suggestions in the teaching plan and the three readings for the lesson.

1. Introduce

ENGAGE PRIOR KNOWLEDGE

Prompt students with questions to discuss what they know about the lesson topic.

TEACH THE SKILL

Introduce the skill using the student-friendly definitions provided for each lesson. These definitions also appear on the Reading 1 page.

2. Model

MODEL THE SKILL

Display Reading 1 on the whiteboard and provide students with a copy. Direct students' attention to the board. Point out the text markings they will be using for the skill as you review the skill definitions.

READ THE PASSAGE

Ask students to follow along as you read aloud the first reading. Tell them to think about the skill and look for it in the text as they read.

MARK THE TEXT

Use the modeling language in the teaching plan to demonstrate how to ask questions about the text and then apply the skill by marking the text on the board. Have students add these marks to their own copy for reference.

3. Practice

PRACTICE THE SKILL

Display Reading 2 on the whiteboard and provide students with a copy. Point out the instructions for text marking.

READ THE PASSAGE

Have students read the passage along with you. Ask them to think about the skill and look for its elements in the text as they read.

MARK THE TEXT

Guide students to mark the skill in the text by asking the comprehension questions provided in the teaching plan.

REVIEW TEXT MARKINGS

Help student volunteers mark the text on the whiteboard.

4. Apply

APPLY THE SKILL
Display Reading 3 on the whiteboard and provide students with a copy. Have them briefly review the text markings before reading.

READ THE PASSAGE
Direct students to read the passage independently. If you think students would benefit, have them read with a partner.

MARK THE TEXT
Ask students to follow the text-marking instructions and monitor their progress as they work independently or with a partner.

REVIEW TEXT MARKINGS
Have several students volunteer to mark the text on the whiteboard. Encourage students to use the academic language of the skill to explain how they marked the text.

CONCLUDE THE LESSON
Wrap up instruction with a prompt that challenges students to apply the topic to their own lives.

Assessment

See the Answer Key on pages 58–63 for annotated versions of each exercise. You may want to be flexible in your assessment of student answers, as the text marks and responses in the annotated exercises do not always represent the only possible answers.

Encourage students to self-assess and correct their answers as you review the text markings on the whiteboard.

Provide additional support to students who need further instruction in the skill by using a fresh copy of the readings.

Read for Details • State Names

1. Introduce

Ask students what they know about state names. Prompt a discussion with these questions: *How did our state get its name? What are some unusual state names?* As they read about state names, students should look for the following:

- The **topic**, or what the text is mostly about.

- The **details**, or important information that tells more about the topic.

- The answers to **questions** such as *who, what, where, when, why,* and *how.*

Continue following the Teaching Routine (pages 8–9) and use the lesson-specific tips for each remaining step.

2. Model

Model for students how to find the topic and supporting details in "Fifty Nifty Names."

- *To find the topic, I'll ask myself what the reading is mostly about. The first sentence says state names come from many places, just like the American people. The rest of the text tells how the states were named. I'll box "State names come from many places" as the topic.*

- *To find important details, I'll look for pieces of information that tell more about the topic. One detail is "27 state names come from Native American words." I'll underline that.*

- *To find details, I'll also look for the answers to questions like* who, what, where, when, why, *and* how.

Materials

- Reading 1: "Fifty Nifty Names" • page 11
- Reading 2: "Native Names" • page 12
- Reading 3: "Kings and Colors" • page 13

3. Practice

Guide students to mark the topic and important details in "Native Names" by asking the following questions.

PARAGRAPH 1:

- *What is this reading mostly about?*
- *What states are named after rivers?*

PARAGRAPH 2:

- *What did two Indian tribes call the Mississippi River?*
- *Who gave the state of Indiana its name?*

4. Apply

Have students complete Reading 3 independently and then share their answers with partners or the group. Conclude by asking: *What questions could you ask to find out important details about your state's name?*

Text-Marking Lessons for Active Nonfiction Reading Grades 4–8 © 2012 by Judith Bauer Stamper, Scholastic Teaching Resources

Read for Details • State Names • 1

When you read for details, remember:

● A **topic** is what a text is mostly about.

● A **detail** is important information that tells more about the topic

● Details answer **questions** such as *who, what, where, when, why,* and *how.*

Read for Details
Text Marks

⬜ Box the **topic**.

〰️ Underline important **details**.

Read "Fifty Nifty Names." Find the topic and important details. Then mark the text.

Fifty Nifty Names

State names come from many places, just like the American people. The Native Americans named many places in North America. That's why 27 state names come from Native American words. What about the other states? Some have the names of kings and queens in Europe. Some have names from other languages. Only one state has the name of an American president. Can you guess which one?

Mark the Text

Find the topic and important details.

⬜ Box the topic.

— Underline how many states are named after Native American words.

Read for Details • State Names • 2

Read "Native Names." Find the topic and important details.
Then mark the text.

Missouri

Native Names

1   Over half our states have Native American names.
Iowa and Missouri are both named after their rivers. How
were the rivers named? The Iowa River takes its name
from the *Ayuwha* or *Iowa* tribe. The Missouri River is named
for the Missouri people. Their name means "people with the
dugout canoes."

2   Connecticut is named after a Mohegan Indian word.
It means "beside the long tidal river." Mississippi's name
comes from several sources. The Algonquin Indians called
the river "messipi." The Chippewa called it "mici zibi." All
the languages agree on one thing. It is a great river. European
settlers made up the name for Indiana. It means "Land of
the Indians."

Mark the Text

1 Find the topic and
important details.

☐ Box the topic.

— Underline what
states are named
after rivers.

2 Find important
details.

— Underline what two
Indian tribes called
the Mississippi
River.

— Underline who
named the state
of Indiana.

Text-Marking Lessons for Active Nonfiction Reading Grades 4–8 © 2012 by Judith Bauer Stamper, Scholastic Teaching Resources

Read for Details • State Names • 3

Read "Kings and Colors." Find the topic and important details.
Then mark the text.

Louisiana

Kings and Colors

1   Explorers and settlers from Europe named about half the states. Several states have royal names. English settlers named Georgia after King George II. A French explorer named Louisiana after King Louis XIV of France. Four states start with "New." New Hampshire, New Jersey, and New York have English names. New Mexico takes its name from its neighbor, Mexico.

2   Several states have colorful names. Colorado means "reddish color" in Spanish. Spanish explorers named it for its reddish rocks. French explorers named Vermont. They loved its tree-covered "green mountains." What state is named after an American president? That's right—Washington!

Mark the Text

1   Find the topic and important details.

☐   Box the topic.

—   Underline which states have royal names.

2   Underline the important details.

—   Who named a state after a reddish color?

—   What state is named after a President?

Text-Marking Lessons for Active Nonfiction Reading Grades 4–8 © 2012 by Judith Bauer Stamper, Scholastic Teaching Resources

Main Idea & Details • Insect Attacks

1. Introduce the Skill

Ask students what they know about insect attacks. Prompt a discussion with these questions: *What insects bite and sting humans? How do insect bites and stings feel?* As they read about insect attacks, students should look for the following:

- The **main idea**, or the most important point about a topic.

- **Supporting details**, or information that tells more about the main idea.

Continue following the Teaching Routine (pages 8–9) and use the lesson-specific tips for each remaining step.

2. Model

Model for students how to find the main idea and supporting details in "Buzz and Bite."

- *To find the main idea, I'll look for the most important point about the topic. The topic is insect attacks. The main idea of this reading is about why mosquitoes bite. I'll circle the second sentence as the main idea.*

- *To find the supporting details, I'll look for pieces of information that tell more about the main idea. One detail is that a female mosquito bites to get blood so she can make more mosquitoes. I'll underline that because it is a supporting detail. Then I'll find more supporting details.*

Materials

- Reading 1: "Buzz and Bite" • page 15
- Reading 2: "That Stings!" • page 16
- Reading 3: "Bad Bug Bites" • page 17

3. Practice

Guide students to mark the main idea and details in "That Stings!" by asking the following questions.

PARAGRAPH 1:

- *What is the main idea about insect attacks in this paragraph?*

- *What is supporting information about a honeybee's sting?*

- *How are wasp stings different?*

PARAGRAPH 2:

- *What is the main idea about insect attacks in this paragraph?*

- *What is supporting information about a bee or wasp sting?*

- *Why do some people get hives and become dizzy?*

4. Apply

Have students complete Reading 3 independently and then share their answers with partners or the group. Conclude by asking: *Which kind of insect would you* least *want to attack you? Why?*

Text-Marking Lessons for Active Nonfiction Reading Grades 4–8 © 2012 by Judith Bauer Stamper, Scholastic Teaching Resources

Name _____   Date _____

Main Idea & Details • Insect Attacks • 1

To find key information as you read, remember:

- The **main idea** is the most important point about a topic.

- **Supporting details** are information that tells more about the main idea.

Main Idea & Details Text Marks

⬭ Circle the **main idea**.

∼ Underline the **supporting details**.

Read "Buzz and Bite." Find the main idea and supporting details. Then mark the text.

Buzz and Bite

People all over the world are scratching their mosquito bites. Why do mosquitoes like to bite? A female mosquito needs blood to make more mosquitoes. The female's mouth has a special part. She uses it to suck blood. She shoots some of her saliva into a person. It makes the blood easier to drink. The mosquito's saliva is what makes a bite itch. Yuk!

Mark the Text

Find the main idea and supporting details.

⬭ Circle the main idea.

∼ Underline the supporting details.

Main Idea & Details • Insect Attacks • 2

Read "That Stings!" Find the main idea and supporting details. Then mark the text.

That Stings!

1   Don't make a bee or wasp mad at you! Bees and wasps fight back with their stingers when they are disturbed or angry. A honeybee can sting a person only once. Its stinger gets stuck inside the victim's body. The honeybee dies after just one sting. Wasps, like hornets and yellow jackets, can pull their stingers out. So, they can sting their victims over and over again.

2   A bee or wasp sting hurts when it happens, and it keeps on hurting. After a sting, the skin becomes hot, turns red, and starts to itch. It's always best to remove the stinger as soon as possible. Some people are very allergic to insect stings. They might get hives, become dizzy, and have problems breathing. A little insect sting can cause big trouble.

Mark the Text

1 Find the main idea and supporting details.

⬭ Circle the main idea.

— Underline the supporting details.

2 Find the main idea and supporting details

⬭ Circle the main idea.

— Underline the supporting details.

Text-Marking Lessons for Active Nonfiction Reading Grades 4–8 © 2012 by Judith Bauer Stamper, Scholastic Teaching Resources

Main Idea & Details • Insect Attacks • 3

Read "Bad Bug Bites." Find the main idea and supporting details. Then mark the text.

Bad Bug Bites

1   Two spiders that live in the United States have poisonous bites. They are the black widow and the brown recluse spiders. A black widow spider has a black, shiny body with a red-orange or yellow mark on its stomach. The brown recluse spider is brown with long, skinny legs. If these spiders bite you, the bite will swell, hurt, and make you feel really sick. Few people die from the spider bites. But if one of these spiders bite you, it's important to see a doctor right away.

2   A deer tick is a tiny insect that can cause a bad disease. The tick attaches its six legs to the skin of a victim and sucks its blood. Humans can get Lyme disease, a hard-to-cure illness, from the bacteria in the tick's bite. If you find a tick on your skin, pull it off with a tweezer. Then take the tick to your doctor to be checked.

Mark the Text

1 Find the main idea and supporting details.

◯ Circle the main idea.

— Underline the supporting details.

2 Find the main idea and supporting details.

◯ Circle the main idea.

— Underline the supporting details.

Text-Marking Lessons for Active Nonfiction Reading Grades 4–8 © 2012 by Judith Bauer Stamper, Scholastic Teaching Resources

---

Sequence of Events • Extreme Survivors

---

1. Introduce the Skill

Ask students what they know about extreme survivors. Prompt a discussion with these questions: *What extreme situations can put people's lives in danger? How can people survive dangerous situations?* As they read about extreme survivors, students should look for the following:

- The **events**, or important things that happen in the text.

- The **sequence**, or the order in which things happen.

- **Signal words** that help explain the order in which things happen, such as *first, next, last, yesterday, tomorrow,* and *finally,* plus times and dates.

Continue following the Teaching Routine (pages 8–9) and use the lesson-specific tips for each remaining step.

2. Model

Model for students how to find a sequence of events in "Tsunami Survivor."

- *First, I'll look for signal words that help me understand the order of events. One is the date "December 26, 2004." I'll put a box around that and box the other signal words.*

- *To identify the events, I'll look for important things that happened, like when Ari was swept out to sea. I'll underline the events.*

- *To find the sequence, I'll ask myself what happened first, next, and last. I'll number the events in the order they happened. The first event is that an earthquake caused a tsunami, which created a 30-foot high wave*

Materials

- Reading 1: "Tsunami Survivor"
  - page 19

- Reading 2: "Air Crash Survivor" • page 20

- Reading 3: "Earthquake Survivor"
  - page 21

that crashed over Ari. The last event is that he was finally rescued by a passing ship.

3. Practice

Guide students to mark the sequence of events in "Air Crash Survivor" by asking the following questions.

- *What signal words tell when events happened?*

- *What important events happened to Juliane Koepcke?*

- *What happened first? What happened next? What happened last?*

4. Apply

Have students complete Reading 3 independently and then share their answers with partners or the group. Conclude by asking: *Which one of these extreme situations would you be more likely to survive?*

Text-Marking Lessons for Active Nonfiction Reading Grades 4–8 © 2012 by Judith Bauer Stamper, Scholastic Teaching Resources

Sequence of Events • Extreme Survivors • 1

To determine the sequence of events as you read, remember:

● **Events** are important things that happen.

● The **sequence** is the order in which things happen.

● **Signal words** help explain the order in which things happen. Examples are *first, next, last, yesterday, tomorrow,* and *finally,* plus times and dates.

Sequence of Events Text Marks

⬭ Box the **signal words**.

﹏ Underline the important **events**.

1-2-3 Number the events in the **sequence** they happened.

Read "Tsunami Survivor." Find the sequence of events. Then mark the text.

Tsunami Survivor

On December 26, 2004, an earthquake under the Indian Ocean caused a terrifying tsunami. Ari Afrizal was building a house when a 30-foot high wall of water crashed over him. Soon after, he was swept out to sea. For an hour, he managed to stay afloat. Then he grabbed hold of a wooden plank. The next day, he climbed aboard a leaky fishing boat. On the boat, Ari ate coconuts that floated by and watched shark fins circle around him. Finally, Ari was rescued by a passing ship. He had survived for an amazing 15 days.

Mark the Text

Find the sequence of events.

⬭ Box the times, dates, and signal words.

﹏ Underline the important events.

1-2-3 Number the events in the sequence they happened.

Text-Marking Lessons for Active Nonfiction Reading Grades 4–8 © 2012 by Judith Bauer Stamper, Scholastic Teaching Resources

Sequence of Events • Extreme Survivors • 2

Read "Air Crash Survivor." Find the sequence of events. Then mark the text.

Air Crash Survivor

In December, 1971, Juliane Koepcke boarded a plane. She was headed for the Amazon rainforest to visit her father. An hour later, a bolt of lightning hit the plane. Then it exploded into pieces in midair. Next, Juliane found herself spinning through the air. She fell more than two miles before landing in the thick jungle.

For the next ten days, Juliane walked through the dangerous rainforest. She followed creeks and rivers. She waded through water filled with crocodiles. At last, she found a hut and was rescued. Later, Juliane learned that she was the only survivor of the crash.

Mark the Text

Find the sequence of events.

☐ Box the times, dates, and signal words.

— Underline the important events.

1-2-3 Number the events in the sequence they happened.

Text-Marking Lessons for Active Nonfiction Reading Grades 4–8 © 2012 by Judith Bauer Stamper, Scholastic Teaching Resources

Sequence of Events • Extreme Survivors • 3

**Read "Earthquake Survivor." Find the sequence of events.
Then mark the text.**

Earthquake Survivor

On January 12, 2010, a strong earthquake shook the city of Port-au-Prince, Haiti. Teenager Darlene Etienne was inside a house that collapsed into rubble. At first, Darlene tried to move. However, she was buried under tons of concrete and steel. Next she screamed for help. No one could hear her voice over all the noises in the city. For 15 days, Darlene stayed alive. She continued to call for help. Then a neighbor heard her voice. He alerted rescuers. Finally, a French rescue team pulled her out of the rubble.

Darlene looked like a ghost. She was barely alive, but she never gave up. She was a true survivor.

Mark the Text

Find the sequence of events.

☐ Box the times, dates, and signal words.

— Underline the important events.

1-2-3 Number the events in the sequence they happened.

Summarize • Amazon Rain Forest

1. Introduce the Skill

Ask students what they know about the Amazon rain forest. Prompt a discussion with these questions: *What would it be like to hike in a rain forest? What plants and animals would you see?* As they read about the Amazon, students should think about the following:

- The **topic**, or what the reading is mostly about.

- The **important details** that tell more about the topic.

- A **summary**, or short statement of the topic and important details of a reading.

Continue following the Teaching Routine (pages 8–9) and use the lesson-specific tips for each remaining step.

2. Model

Model for students how to summarize "The Amazon Amazon."

- *First, I'll find the topic, or what the reading is mostly about. I'll circle "The Amazon is the largest tropical rain forest in the world."*

- *Next, I'll check important details that tell about the topic. One important detail is that the Amazon covers about 40 percent of South America.*

- *To summarize, I'll put together a short statement about the topic and important details in my own words. I'll write, "The Amazon, in South America, is the world's largest rain forest. It is warm, rainy, and full of many different plants and animals."*

Materials
■ Reading 1: "The Amazing Amazon" • page 23
■ Reading 2: "Amazon Journey" • page 24
■ Reading 3: "A Rain Forest in Trouble" • page 25

3. Practice

Guide students to summarize "Amazon Journey" by asking the following questions.

- *Who is this reading about?*

- *What did Ed Stafford accomplish?*

- *Why did Stafford make his journey through the Amazon?*

- *How can you use your own words to summarize the reading?*

4. Apply

Have students complete Reading 3 independently and then share their answers with partners or the group. Conclude by asking: *Would you hike in the Amazon? Why or why not?*

Text-Marking Lessons for Active Nonfiction Reading Grades 4–8 © 2012 by Judith Bauer Stamper, Scholastic Teaching Resources

Name _____   Date _____

Summarize • Amazon Rain Forest • 1

To summarize a passage you have read, remember:

● The **topic** is what the reading is mostly about.

● The **important details** tell more about the topic.

● A **summary** is a short statement of the topic and important details of a reading.

> **Summarize Text Marks**
>
> ⬯ Circle the **topic**.
>
> ✓ Check important **details**.
>
> ✎ Write a **summary** in your own words.

Read "The Amazing Amazon." Find the topic and important details. Then mark the text and write a summary.

The Amazing Amazon

The Amazon is the largest tropical rain forest in the world. It covers about 40 percent of South America. Rain forests are in very warm parts of the earth. They also get a rainfall of at least 100 inches each year. Rain forests are home to a huge variety of living things. The Amazon has the most species of plants and animals of any place in the world.

> **Mark the Text**
>
> Summarize the text.
>
> ⬯ Circle the topic.
>
> ✓ Check important details.
>
> ✎ Write a summary in your own words on the lines.

_____

_____

_____

Summarize • Amazon Rain Forest • **2**

Read "Amazon Journey." Find the topic and important details. Then mark the text and write a summary.

Amazon Journey

Many people want to protect the Amazon rain forest. But few care as much as Ed Stafford. Stafford is the first person to ever hike the entire length of the Amazon River. Stafford started at the river's source in Peru. He ended where the river flows into the ocean in Brazil. The journey stretched for 4,200 miles through the rain forest.

Along the way, Stafford waded through dangerous waters. They were full of hungry piranha fish and crocodiles. On land, he met snakes, jaguars, and millions of mosquitoes. Almost two and a half years later, Stafford finished his hike. He did it to call the world's attention to saving the Amazon.

Mark the Text

Summarize the text.

◯ Circle the topic.

✓ Check important details.

✐ Write a summary in your own words on the lines.

_____

_____

_____

Text-Marking Lessons for Active Nonfiction Reading Grades 4–8 © 2012 by Judith Bauer Stamper, Scholastic Teaching Resources

Summarize • Amazon Rain Forest • 3

Read "A Rain Forest in Trouble." Find the topic and important details. Then mark the text and write a summary.

A Rain Forest in Trouble

Even though it is a huge place, the Amazon is in trouble. In just a few decades, the Amazon has lost almost 17 percent of its trees. Experts worry what will happen next. They predict that 55 percent of the Amazon might be destroyed by 2030.

Humans are destroying the Amazon for their own use. Farmers clear land to raise cattle and crops. Loggers cut down trees to make cheap timber. Roads, mines, and gas lines all add to the problem.

Other people are working hard to save the Amazon. Rain forests are the source of many foods and medicines. Rain forests absorb carbon dioxide, release oxygen, and keep the planet healthy. Saving the Amazon means saving the planet.

Mark the Text

Summarize the text.

- ⬭ Circle the topic.
- ✓ Check important details.
- ✏ Write a summary in your own words on the lines.

_____

_____

_____

Text-Marking Lessons for Active Nonfiction Reading Grades 4–8 © 2012 by Judith Bauer Stamper, Scholastic Teaching Resources

Cause & Effect • Volcanoes

1. Introduce the Skill

Ask students what they know about volcanoes. Prompt a discussion with these questions: *What does an erupting volcano look like? What happens as a result of a volcanic eruption?* As they read about volcanoes, students should look for the following:

- A **cause**, or a reason something happened.

- An **effect**, or what happened as a result.

- **Signal words** that help identify the cause and effect. Examples are *therefore, as a result, because, so,* and *for this reason*.

Continue following the Teaching Routine (pages 8–9) and use the lesson-specific tips for each remaining step.

2. Model

Model for students how to find a cause and effect relationship in "Mount St. Helens Blows Up!"

- *To find the cause, I'll ask, "Why did it happen?" The text says a violent eruption caused the mountain to explode and shoot out lava, rocks, ash, and gas. I'll circle that sentence because it is the cause.*

- *I see the signal words* as a result. *I'll draw a box around the words because they tell me that an effect is next.*

- *To find the effect, I'll ask "What happened as a result?" It says that 57 people died and countless animals and plants were destroyed. I'll underline that because it is the effect.*

Materials

- Reading 1: "Mount St. Helens Blows Up!"
  - page 27

- Reading 2: "When Volcanoes Explode"
  - page 28

- Reading 3: "Ash From Iceland" • page 29

3. Practice

Guide students to mark the cause-and-effect relationships in "When Volcanoes Explode" by asking the following questions.

PARAGRAPH 1:

- *What happens when a volcano explodes?*

- *What signal word tells you there is a cause-and-effect relationship?*

- *What happens as a result of the fiery lava?*

PARAGRAPH 2:

- *What do the clouds of ash do?*

- *What signal word tells you there is a cause-and-effect relationship?*

- *What are two effects that are a result of the exploding ash?*

4. Apply

Have students complete Reading 3 independently and then share their answers with partners or the group. Conclude by asking: *If you heard that a volcano was about to explode nearby, what effect would it have on you?*

Text-Marking Lessons for Active Nonfiction Reading Grades 4–8 © 2012 by Judith Bauer Stamper, Scholastic Teaching Resources

Cause & Effect • Volcanoes • 1

To identify cause and effect as you read, remember:

● A **cause** is the reason something happened.

● An **effect** is what happened as a result.

● **Signal words** help identify the cause and effect. Examples are *therefore, as a result, because, so,* and *for this reason*.

Cause & Effect Text Marks

⬭ Circle the **cause**.

▱ Box the **signal word**.

— Underline the **effect**.

Read "Mount St. Helens Blows Up!" Find a cause-and-effect relationship. Then mark the text.

Mount St. Helens Blows Up!

Mount St. Helens is a volcano in the state of Washington. For many years, it was inactive. Then, in 1980, it started to show signs of life. On May 18, the volcano blew up. A violent eruption caused the mountain to explode and shoot out lava, rocks, ash, and gas. As a result of the eruption, 57 people died and countless animals and plants were destroyed. It was the deadliest eruption ever in the United States.

Mark the Text

Find a cause-and- effect relationship.

⬭ Circle the cause.

▱ Box the signal word.

— Underline the effect.

Text-Marking Lessons for Active Nonfiction Reading Grades 4–8 © 2012 by Judith Bauer Stamper, Scholastic Teaching Resources

Cause & Effect • Volcanoes • 2

Read "When Volcanoes Explode" Find the cause-and-effect relationships. Then mark the text.

When Volcanoes Explode

1   When a volcano explodes, it destroys everything around it. Lava—red hot, melted rock—spurts out of the top. Because the lava is so hot and thick, it burns everything in its path. That includes trees, houses, and even cars. The lava turns into hard rock when it cools.

2   An erupting volcano also shoots out huge clouds of ash mixed with poisonous gases. Sometimes, the clouds of ash are so thick and high that they block out the sun. As a result, the climate of the area can grow cooler. Thick ash clouds are also a danger to jet planes. The ash can make a plane crash by clogging up its engines.

   If you are ever near an erupting volcano, don't waste time. Run for your life!

Mark the Text

1 Find a cause-and-effect relationship.

◯ Circle the cause.

▭ Box the signal word.

— Underline the effect.

2 Find a cause-and-effect relationship.

◯ Circle the cause.

▭ Box the signal words.

— Underline two effects.

Text-Marking Lessons for Active Nonfiction Reading Grades 4–8 © 2012 by Judith Bauer Stamper, Scholastic Teaching Resources

Cause & Effect • Volcanoes • 3

Read "Ash From Iceland." Find the cause-and-effect relationships. Mark the text.

Ash From Iceland

1   In the spring of 2010, a volcano in Iceland made world headlines. The volcano's name is Eyjafjallajökull. It sits under a large ice cap near the Arctic Circle. The volcano began to erupt in late March. Its fiery heat melted the ice above it, causing rivers to flood and forcing residents to evacuate.

2   Things really started to heat up on April 14. The volcano shot up clouds containing millions of fine pieces of glassy ash. The ash drifted high into the air over Europe. As a result, governments would not allow planes to take off or land. Millions of travelers were stranded in airports. Almost a week passed before the airports opened again. A small volcano showed the world the power of nature.

Mark the Text

1   Find a cause-and-effect relationship.

◯   Circle the cause.

▱   Box the signal word.

—   Underline two effects.

2   Find a cause-and-effect relationship.

◯   Circle the cause.

▱   Box the signal words.

—   Underline two effects.

Draw Conclusions • Sports Stars

1. Introduce the Skill

Ask students what they know about famous sports stars. Prompt a discussion with these questions: *Who do you think is a top sports star of all time? What characteristics do you think these sports stars share?* As they read about sports stars, students should do the following:

- Look for **facts** that tell them information about the topic.
- **Think about** the facts and combine them to come to a new understanding.
- **Draw a conclusion** about the topic.

Continue following the Teaching Routine (pages 8–9) and use the lesson-specific tips for each remaining step.

2. Model

Model for students how to draw a conclusion about "Wilma Rudolph."

- *To draw a conclusion about Wilma Rudolph's character, I'll look for facts about her. I'll underline that she had polio as a child. I'll also underline that she was able to walk again by age 12 and that she won three Olympic medals eight years later.*
- *I'll combine all these facts and think about what they tell me about Wilma Rudolph.*
- *I'll draw the conclusion that Wilma Rudolph must have been a very determined, hard-working person. I'll write that on the lines under the text.*

Materials

- Reading 1: "Wilma Rudolph" • page 31
- Reading 2: "Bruce Lee" • page 32
- Reading 3: "Pele" • page 33

3. Practice

Guide students to draw a conclusion about "Bruce Lee" by asking the following questions.

PARAGRAPH 1:

- *What facts did you learn about how Bruce Lee became a marital arts expert?*
- *What new understanding do you have about Bruce Lee when you put these facts together?*
- *Draw a conclusion about how he became an expert so quickly.*

PARAGRAPH 2:

- *What different kinds of skills did Bruce Lee have?*
- *What does this tell you about him?*
- *Draw a conclusion about Bruce Lee's character.*

4. Apply

Have students complete Reading 3 independently and then share their answers with partners or the group. Conclude by asking: *What do these three sports stars have in common?*

Text-Marking Lessons for Active Nonfiction Reading Grades 4–8 © 2012 by Judith Bauer Stamper, Scholastic Teaching Resources

Draw Conclusions • Sports Stars • 1

To draw conclusions based on what you read, remember:

● A **conclusion** is a new understanding about a topic.

● Text **facts** tell you information about the topic.

● **Think about** the facts and combine them to draw a conclusion.

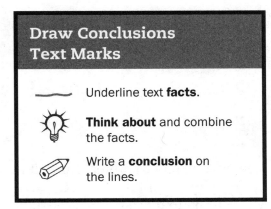

Draw Conclusions Text Marks

——— Underline text **facts**.

Think about and combine the facts.

Write a **conclusion** on the lines.

Read "Wilma Rudolph." Mark the text and draw a conclusion.

Wilma Rudolph

People called her "the fastest woman in history." In 1960, Wilma Rudolph won three gold medals at a single Olympics. It was a great achievement for any athlete. For Rudolph, it was amazing. She had polio as a child. The disease left her left leg paralyzed. With the help of doctors, Rudolph walked again by age 12. Only eight years later, she went to the Olympics and ran off with the gold.

Mark the Text

Draw a conclusion: What sort of person was Wilma Rudolph?

——— Underline text facts.

 Think about and combine the facts.

 Write a conclusion on the lines.

_____

_____

_____

Draw Conclusions • Sports Stars • 2

Read "Bruce Lee." Mark the text and draw conclusions.

Bruce Lee

1   Bruce Lee was weak and sickly as a child. As a teenager, he had to protect himself in his tough neighborhood. So, he took up martial arts. Lee studied every kind of physical fighting. He worked out constantly. He did sit-ups while watching TV. He practiced kicks while walking down the street. He quickly became a master of the martial arts.

_____

_____

2   Bruce Lee made martial arts popular in the United States. He amazed audiences with his karate and kung fu skills. He wrote and directed martial arts movies and starred in them himself. He became the highest paid actor in the world, as well as an amazing athlete. Because of Bruce Lee, millions of U.S. kids became fans of the martial arts.

_____

_____

Mark the Text

1   Draw a conclusion: How did Bruce Lee learn martial arts so quickly?

___   Underline text facts.

💡   Use logic to think about the facts.

✏️   Write a conclusion on the lines.

2   Draw a conclusion: What do all Bruce Lee's accomplishments tell you about him?

___   Underline text facts.

💡   Use logic to think about the facts.

✏️   Write a conclusion on the lines.

Text-Marking Lessons for Active Nonfiction Reading Grades 4–8 © 2012 by Judith Bauer Stamper, Scholastic Teaching Resources

Draw Conclusions • Sports Stars • 3

Read "Pele." Mark the text and draw conclusions.

Pele

1   Who is the most famous soccer star of all time? Most people will answer with just one name—Pele. Pele grew up in Brazil. He kicked a grapefruit around as his first soccer ball. Next he practiced with an old sock stuffed with newspapers. Then he started to play with a real soccer ball in school. People knew right away that he was a star.

_____

_____

2   At 17, Pele's amazing talent put him on Brazil's World Cup team. He scored the only goals in Brazil's World Cup victory. One goal was his famous "bicycle" kick backwards. Years later, Brazilians watched as Pele kicked his one thousandth goal. The crowd cheered their hero for 11 minutes!

_____

_____

Mark the Text

1 Draw a conclusion: What kind of childhood did Pele have?

— Underline text facts.

💡 Use logic to think about the facts.

✏️ Write a conclusion on the lines.

2 Draw a conclusion: How popular was Pele in Brazil?

— Underline text facts.

💡 Use logic to think about the facts.

✏️ Write a conclusion on the lines.

Problem & Solution • Rescue Teams

1. Introduce the Skill

Ask students what they know about rescue teams. Prompt a discussion with these questions: *What kind of emergencies require special rescue teams? How do rescue teams operate?* As they read about rescue teams, students should look for the following:

- A **problem**, or a difficult situation that needs to be fixed.

- A **solution**, or way of dealing with a problem or difficulty.

- **Signal words** that describe the problem and solution, such as *problem, challenge, solve, fix,* and *solution.*

Continue following the Teaching Routine (pages 8–9) and use the lesson-specific tips for each remaining step.

2. Model

Model for students how to find a problem and solution in "Buried Alive!"

- *First, I'll look for signal words that give me clues about the problem and solution. I'll box* challenge *and* solve *the problem.*

- *To find the problem, I'll look for the difficult situation that has to be fixed. The text says that it's a huge challenge to rescue people buried under the rubble. I'll circle that sentence.*

- *To find the solution, I'll look for how the problem was solved. I read three ways that the rescuers solve the problem. I'll underline all three parts of the solution.*

Materials

- Reading 1: "Buried Alive!" • page 35

- Reading 2: "Air Lifts" • page 36

- Reading 3: "Animal Emergencies" • page 37

3. Practice

Guide students to mark the problem and solution in "Air Lifts" by asking the following questions.

PARAGRAPH 1:

- *What signal words give you clues about the problem and solution?*

- *What problem can an avalanche cause?*

- *What is the solution?*

PARAGRAPH 2:

- *What signal words give you clues about the problem and solution?*

- *What problem can flash floods cause?*

- *How can the problem be solved?*

4. Apply

Have students complete Reading 3 independently and then share their answers with partners or the group. Conclude by asking: *What news stories have you heard that describe human and animal rescues?*

Text-Marking Lessons for Active Nonfiction Reading Grades 4–8 © 2012 by Judith Bauer Stamper, Scholastic Teaching Resources

Problem & Solution • Rescue Teams • 1

To help you identify a problem or solution as you read, remember:

- A **problem** is a difficult situation that needs to be fixed.

- A **solution** is a way of dealing with a problem or difficulty.

- **Signal words** such as *problem, challenge, solve, fix,* and *solution* help describe the problem and solution.

Problem & Solution Text Marks

☐ Box the **signal word**.

◯ Circle the **problem**.

~ Underline the **solution**.

Read "Buried Alive!" Find a problem and solution. Then mark the text.

Buried Alive!

An earthquake sends shock waves through the ground. Buildings fall down into piles of rubble. Rescuing people buried under the rubble is a huge challenge. Rescue teams have special ways to solve the problem. They use microphones to hear the victims. They use dogs to locate them. Then they tunnel through the rubble to pull out the survivors.

Mark the Text

Find the problem and the solution.

☐ Box the signal words.

◯ Circle the problem.

~ Underline the solution.

Problem & Solution • Rescue Teams • 2

Read "Air Lifts." Find the problems and solutions. Then mark the text.

Air Lifts

1   In an avalanche, snow comes crashing down a mountain. People in the way face a terrible problem. They are buried under a ton of snow. How do they survive? Mountain rescue teams solve the problem. They fly helicopters into the area. They find survivors by radio signals or rescue dogs. Then they dig out the victims. Sometimes, there are just minutes to spare.

2   Heavy rains cause flash floods. With little warning, people are trapped in their houses by floodwaters. There is no way to walk, drive, or swim away. Helicopters solve the problem by flying into flood areas. Rescuers lift people off their roofs and carry them to safety.

Mark the Text

1   Find the problem and the solution.

▱   Box the signal words.

◯   Circle the problem.

—   Underline the solution.

2   Find the problem and the solution.

▱   Box the signal words.

◯   Circle the problem.

—   Underline the solution.

Text-Marking Lessons for Active Nonfiction Reading Grades 4–8 © 2012 by Judith Bauer Stamper, Scholastic Teaching Resources

Problem & Solution • Rescue Teams • 3

Read "Animal Emergencies." Find the problems and solutions. Then mark the text.

Animal Emergencies

1   Even animals need special rescues. Every year, a number of whales lose their way in the ocean. They become stranded on beaches. It's a big problem to get them back into the water. Rescue teams fix the problem with a crane. They lift up the whale in a big canvas sling. Then they drop it back into the ocean.

2   Oil slicks are a deadly problem for coastal birds. When oil coats the birds' feathers, they can't fly or clean themselves. Rescuers solve the problem by cleaning the feathers with a special chemical. Then they return the birds to their homes in nature.

Mark the Text

1   Find the problem and the solution.

▱   Box the signal words.

◯   Circle the problem.

—   Underline the solution.

2   Find the problem and the solution.

▱   Box the signal words.

◯   Circle the problem.

—   Underline the solution.

Compare & Contrast • Predator Power

1. Introduce the Skill

Ask students what they know about vampire bats and great white sharks. Prompt a discussion with these questions: *How are vampire bats different from other bats? How are great white sharks like other sharks? How are they different?* As they read about powerful predators, students should do the following:

- **Compare**, or tell how two or more things are alike.

- **Contrast**, or tell how two or more things are different.

- Look for **signal words** such as *both, too, like, alike, different, in addition, but, rather, than,* and *however.*

Continue following the Teaching Routine (pages 8–9) and use the lesson-specific tips for each remaining step.

2. Model

Model for students how to find comparisons and contrasts in "Komodo Dragons."

- *To compare, I'll ask myself how two things are the same. I'll look for signal words such as* both, too, alike, *and* in addition. *I'll circle the sentences that tell how the Komodo dragon and other lizards have scaly skin and lay eggs to have their young. I'll box the signal words* like *and* also.

- *To contrast, I'll ask myself how two things are different. I'll look for signal words such as* but, rather, than, however, *and* different. *I'll underline the sentences that tell how*

Materials

- Reading 1: "Komodo Dragons" • page 39
- Reading 2: "Vampire Bats" • page 40
- Reading 3: "Great White Sharks" • page 41

Komodo dragons are bigger and eat more than other lizards. I'll box the signal words however *and* different.

3. Practice

Guide students to mark the comparisons and contrasts in "Vampire Bats" by asking the following questions.

PARAGRAPH 1:

- *How are vampire bats like other bats?*

- *What signal words help describe the comparisons?*

PARAGRAPH 2:

- *How are vampire bats different from other bats?*

- *What signal words help describe the contrasts?*

4. Apply

Have students complete Reading 3 independently and then share their answers with partners or the group. Conclude by asking: *Which of the powerful predators do you find most frightening?*

Text-Marking Lessons for Active Nonfiction Reading Grades 4–8 © 2012 by Judith Bauer Stamper, Scholastic Teaching Resources

Compare & Contrast • Predator Power • 1

To help you compare and contrast information as you read, remember:

- To **compare** means to tell how two or more things are the same.

- To **contrast** means to tell how two or more things are different.

- **Signal words** help describe a comparisons or a contrast. Examples are *both, too, like, alike, different, also, in addition, but, rather than,* and *however*.

Compare & Contrast Text Marks

- ⬭ To **compare**, circle ways that things are the same.

- ﹏ To **contrast**, underline ways that things are different

- ▭ Box the **signal words**.

Read "Komodo Dragons." Compare and contrast Komodo dragons with other lizards. Then mark the text.

Komodo Dragons

The world of lizards is full of strange, scaly animals, but one lizard stands out from the rest. It is called the Komodo dragon. Like other lizards, Komodo dragons have scaly skin. They also lays eggs to have their young like other lizards. However, Komodo dragons are much bigger than other lizards. They can weigh up to three hundred pounds. The amount they eat is different, as well. They can finish off several wild pigs for lunch.

Mark the Text

Compare and contrast Komodo dragons with other lizards.

- ⬭ Circle two ways they are the same.

- ﹏ Underline two ways they are different.

- ▭ Box the signal words.

Compare & Contrast • Predator Power • 2

Read "Vampire Bats." Compare and contrast vampire bats with other bats. Then mark the text.

Vampire Bats

1   Many people find bats a little creepy. One kind of bat is really creepy. It is called a vampire bat. Like other bats, the vampire bat is a mammal. A mammal is covered by hair or fur and gives birth to live babies. Vampire bats are also like other bats in where they live. They hang out in dark places like caves, and they sleep during the day and fly at night.

2   However, there are big differences between vampire bats and other bats. Most bats eat insects or small animals like mice. A vampire bat is different in what it eats. It feeds entirely on blood! Vampire bats bite livestock like cows and lap up their blood for half an hour. How can you recognize a vampire bat? Its teeth are different from those of other bats. They are longer and sharper. Creepy!

Mark the Text

1 Compare vampire bats with other bats.

◯ Circle two ways they are the same.

▢ Box the signal words.

2 Contrast vampire bats with other bats.

— Underline two ways they are different.

▢ Box the signal words.

Text-Marking Lessons for Active Nonfiction Reading Grades 4–8 © 2012 by Judith Bauer Stamper, Scholastic Teaching Resources

Compare & Contrast • Predator Power • 3

Read "Great White Sharks." Compare and contrast great white sharks with other sharks. Then mark the text.

Great White Sharks

1 Do sharks deserve their bloodthirsty reputation? One shark—the great white shark—deserves all the respect it gets. Like all sharks, great white sharks have no bones. Instead of bones, shark skeletons are made of cartilage, which is like the end of a human nose. In addition, great whites and other sharks both have many rows of teeth that fall out and grow back easily.

2 The great white shark is different from other sharks in its size. It is the largest predator in the sea. It can grow up to 20 feet long and weigh up to 4,500 pounds. The great white is also different from other sharks in its feeding habits. It is the most vicious hunter. It often attacks its prey from below, ripping it apart in its huge jaws. If you see the fin of a great white shark, it's time to get out of the water!

Mark the Text

1 Compare great white sharks with other sharks.

⬭ Circle two ways they are the same.

▭ Box the signal words.

2 Contrast great white sharks with other sharks.

— Underline two ways they are different.

▭ Box the signal words.

Text-Marking Lessons for Active Nonfiction Reading Grades 4–8 © 2012 by Judith Bauer Stamper, Scholastic Teaching Resources

Make Inferences • Record Breakers

1. Introduce the Skill

Ask students what they know about people who set world records. Prompt a discussion with these questions: *What world records can you name? What kind of people are able to set a world record?* As they read about record breakers, students should do the following:

- Ask if there is an **idea** the author hints at, but doesn't state directly.
- Look for **text clues** that help them figure out the unstated idea.
- Combine the text clues with their own **knowledge and experience**.
- **Make an inference** about something that isn't stated in the text.

Continue following the Teaching Routine (pages 8–9) and use the lesson-specific tips for each remaining step.

2. Model

Model for students how to make an inference about "Champion Skippers."

- *First, I'll ask a question about the text. The author talks about "Double-Dutch style skips," but doesn't state what they are. What does "Double Dutch" mean?*
- *To find text clues, I'll look for information that hints at the meaning of Double Dutch. It says that five Skippers competed and that three girls and two boys set a new record. I'll underline that.*
- *To use my own knowledge and experience, I'll think about seeing a team of girls jumping rope together. I think it was called Double Dutch.*

Materials

- Reading 1: "Champion Skippers" • page 43
- Reading 2: "Youngest Climber" • page 44
- Reading 3: "Wheelchair Champ" • page 45

- *To make a inference, I'll combine the text clues with my experience. I'll write, "Double Dutch means that a team of jumpers jump rope at the same time."*

3. Practice

Guide students to make an inference about "Youngest Climber" by asking the following questions.

- *Why do some people think it was wrong for Jordan to climb Mt. Everest?*
- *What text clues give you a hint?*
- *What can you add from your own knowledge?*
- *What inference can you make?*

4. Apply

Have students complete Reading 3 independently and then share their answers with partners or the group. Conclude by asking: *If someone told you she wanted to set a world record for bicycling across the country, what inference would you make about her?*

Text-Marking Lessons for Active Nonfiction Reading Grades 4–8 © 2012 by Judith Bauer Stamper, Scholastic Teaching Resources

Make Inferences • Record Breakers • 1

To help you make inferences as you read, remember:

● An **inference** is a combination of text clues and what you already know.

● A **text clue** is a key word or detail that helps a reader figure out an unstated idea.

● **Background knowledge** is what you already know about a topic.

> **Make Inferences Text Marks**
>
> ‿‿‿ Underline **text clues**.
>
> Think about **what you already know**.
>
> Write an **inference** on the lines.

Read "Champion Skippers." Find text clues and combine them with your own knowledge to make an inference. Then mark the text.

Champion Skippers

The Summerville Skippers are a jump rope group from Boise, Idaho. They won the World Championship Title for Team USA. That title is equal to the Olympics of Jump Rope. In 2010, five Skippers competed in a Guinness World Records Day celebration. The three girls and two boys set a new record for Double-Dutch style skips. What was their record-breaking number? It was 371 skips in a row!

> **Mark the Text**
>
> Make an inference: What is "Double Dutch" jump rope?
>
> ‿‿‿ Underline text clues.
>
> Think about what you already know.
>
> Write your inference on the lines.

_____

_____

_____

Make Inferences • Record Breakers • 2

Read "Youngest Climber." Find text clues and combine them with your own knowledge to make an inference. Then mark the text.

Youngest Climber

In May 2010, 13-year-old Jordan Romero set a world record. Even more amazing, he did it on top of the world! Jordan climbed to the summit of Mount Everest. It is the highest mountain in the world. He became the youngest person ever to climb Everest.

Jordan made the climb with his father, his mother, and three Sherpas. Jordan hopes to climb the Seven Summits. Those are the highest points on all seven continents. Reactions to Jordan's climb were mixed. Many people think he is a hero. Others think a 13-year-old shouldn't be on Everest. Every year, climbers die on the mountain. One thing is for sure, Jordan is a top teen athlete.

Mark the Text

Make an inference: Why do some people think it was wrong for Jordan to climb Mt. Everest?

—— Underline text clues.

 Think about what you already know.

✏ Write your inference on the lines.

_____

_____

_____

Text-Marking Lessons for Active Nonfiction Reading Grades 4–8 © 2012 by Judith Bauer Stamper, Scholastic Teaching Resources

Make Inferences • Record Breakers • 3

Read "Wheelchair Champ." Find text clues and combine them with your own knowledge to make an inference. Then mark the text.

Wheelchair Champ

Aaron Fotheringham is a true champ. He was born with spina bifida. The disease paralyzed him from the waist down. But getting around in a wheelchair hasn't stopped Aaron. When he was just 8, he went to a skateboard park. Ten years later, he is a record-setter on his wheelchair skateboard.

In 2008, Aaron landed a single back flip in his wheelchair. Right away, Aaron set a new goal for himself. He would try a double back flip. Aaron attempted the trick over and over again. Finally, in 2010, Aaron did it. He flew off a ramp, landed a double back flip, and went into the record books.

What does a champ do next? Aaron is working with disabled children. He hopes to inspire them to reach their own dreams.

Mark the Text

Make an inference: Why do you think Aaron has become a champ?

_____ Underline text clues.

 Think about what you already know.

 Write your inference on the lines.

_____

_____

_____

Fact and Opinion • Up for Debate

1. Introduce the Skill

Ask students what they know about debates. Prompt a discussion with these questions: *Are you for or against girls playing on boys' sports teams? Would you vote yes or no to allow cell phones in classrooms?* As they read about debate issues, students should look for the following:

- A **fact**, or a statement that can be proven true.

- An **opinion**, or a statement of someone's personal feeling or belief.

- **Signal words**, such as *believe, think, feel,* and *unfair,* which can help them recognize an opinion.

Continue following the Teaching Routine (pages 8–9) and use the lesson-specific tips for each remaining step.

2. Model

Model for students how to identify facts and opinions in "Should Students Go to School Year-Round?"

- *To identify a fact, I'll ask "Can this statement be proven true? Where or how would I check whether it's true?" I'll circle the statement, "In Germany and Japan, students go to school year-round." That is a fact because I can prove that it's true by checking in an encyclopedia or on the Internet. I'll also circle the sentence that begins, "In the United States . . . ."*

- *To identify an opinion, I'll ask, "Is this someone's belief, feeling, or judgment?" I'll also look for signal words, such as think, believe, best, worst, fair, and unfair. I'll underline the sentence that begins with*

Materials
■ Reading 1: "Should Students Go to School Year-Round?" • page 47
■ Reading 2: "Should Girls Play on Boys' Sports Teams?" • page 48
■ Reading 3: "Should Cell Phones Be Allowed in School?" • page 49

"Some experts believe . . ." because that is an opinion. It has the signal word *believe and* tells what someone thinks. I'll box *believe. I'll also underline the sentence that begins "However, many parents think . . ." and box* think.

3. Practice

Guide students to mark the facts and opinions in "Should Girls Play on Boys' Sports Teams?" by asking the following questions.

- *What are two statements that are facts?*

- *How could you check to see that they are true?*

- *What are two statements that are opinions?*

- *What signal words tell you that they are opinions?*

4. Apply

Have students complete Reading 3 independently and then share their answers with partners or the group. Conclude by asking: *What is an issue that you have a strong opinion about?*

Text-Marking Lessons for Active Nonfiction Reading Grades 4–8 • © 2012 by Judith Bauer Stamper, Scholastic Teaching Resources

Fact & Opinion • Up for Debate • 1

To tell fact from opinion as you read, remember:

● A **fact** is a statement that can be proved to be true.

● An **opinion** is a statement of someone's personal belief or feeling.

● **Signal words**, such as *believe, think, feel,* and *unfair* help you recognize an opinion.

**Facts & Opinion
Text Marks**

⬭ Circle a **fact**.

⎯ Underline an **opinion**.

▱ Box the **signal word**.

**Read "Should Students Go to School Year-Round?"
Identify facts and opinions. Then mark the text.**

Should Students Go to School Year-Round?

In Germany and Japan, students go to school year-round. In the United States, students have two or more month's vacation. Should American students to be in class 12 months a year?

Some experts believe that summer vacation hurts education. They say students forget what they have learned. However, many parents think that kids need a break from school. Who do you think is right?

Mark the Text

Identify facts and opinions.

⬭ Circle two facts.

⎯ Underline two opinions.

▱ Box the signal words.

Fact & Opinion • Up for Debate • 2

Read "Should Girls Play on Boys' Sports Teams?" Identify facts and opinions. Then mark the text.

Should Girls Play On Boys' Sports Teams?

In 1972, Congress passed a law called Title IX. It states that girls and boys should have equal opportunities in school. The law changed school sports forever. The number of girls playing high school sports grew from 30,000 in 1972 to over 170,000 today. Many girls now want to play on boys' sports teams.

Some people think that a girl playing on a boys' team is wrong. They say girls are weaker and could get hurt. They argue that it's not fair to the boys on the teams. Other people believe that girls have as much right to play as boys. If a girl is good enough to make a team, she should be able to play on it. There are strong opinions on both sides of the issue.

Mark the Text

Identify facts and opinions.

◯ Circle two facts.

— Underline two opinions.

▭ Box the signal words.

Text-Marking Lessons for Active Nonfiction Reading Grades 4–8 © 2012 by Judith Bauer Stamper, Scholastic Teaching Resources

Fact & Opinion • Up for Debate • 3

**Read "Should Cell Phones Be Allowed in School?"
Identify facts and opinions. Then mark the text.**

Should Cell Phones Be Allowed in School?

A recent survey shows that 75 percent of teens between ages 12 and 17 have their own cell phones. They carry them everywhere, including to school. That has caused a big debate. Kids use their cell phones to talk, to text, and to take pictures. However, problems come up when kids have cell phones in schools. Over two-thirds of high schools have banned cell phones.

Many teachers believe that cell phones interfere with learning. Kids might check their phones for text messages. A call can disrupt a class. Many parents feel their kids should carry cell phones. They like being able to get in touch with their kids. They think the phones keep their kids safe.

What do you think? Should kids have cell phones in school?

Mark the Text

Identify facts and opinions.

◯   Circle two facts.

—   Underline two opinions.

▭   Box the signal words.

Text-Marking Lessons for Active Nonfiction Reading Grades 4–8 © 2012 by Judith Bauer Stamper, Scholastic Teaching Resources

Context Clues • Good as Gold

1. Introduce the Skill

Ask students what they know about gold. Prompt a discussion with these questions: *Why is gold so valuable? How do people find gold and mine it?* As they read about gold, students should look for the following:

- An **unfamiliar word**, or a word they don't know the meaning of.
- The **context**, or words and sentences around the unfamiliar word.
- **Context clues**, or specific clues in the sentences that can reveal the meaning of the unfamiliar word.

Continue following the Teaching Routine (pages 8–9) and use the lesson-specific tips for each remaining step.

2. Model

Model for students how to use context clues to find the meaning of an unfamiliar word in "A Precious Metal."

- *I'll circle the word* rare *as an unfamiliar word to learn more about.*
- *To find context clues, I'll look in the sentences where the word appears, and in the sentences around it. I'll underline the words "very little gold on Earth" and the sentence that compares the amount of gold to the amount of dirt.*
- *To identify the meaning of* rare, *I'll put together the clues and write its meaning.* Rare *means something uncommon or unusual.*

Materials

- ■ Reading 1: "A Precious Metal" • page 51
- ■ Reading 2: "Hidden Treasure" • page 52
- ■ Reading 3: "Panning for Gold" • page 53

3. Practice

Guide students to use context clues to find the meaning of unfamiliar words in "Hidden Treasure" by asking the following questions.

PARAGRAPH 1:

- *What does the word* seam *mean in this reading?*
- *What context clues can you find for the meaning of* seam?
- *How would you describe the meaning of* seam *in this context?*

PARAGRAPH 2:

- *What does the word* transported *mean in this reading?*
- *What context clues can you find for the meaning of* transported?
- *How would you describe the meaning of* transported *in this context?*

4. Apply

Have students complete Reading 3 independently and then share their answers with partners or the group. Conclude by asking: *What does the idiom "worth its weight in gold" mean? Where do you think it got its meaning?*

Text-Marking Lessons for Active Nonfiction Reading Grades 4–8 © 2012 by Judith Bauer Stamper, Scholastic Teaching Resources

Context Clues • Good as Gold • 1

To understand the meaning of unfamiliar words as you read, remember:

● An **unfamiliar word** is a word that you don't know the meaning of.

● **Context** refers to the words and sentences around the unfamiliar word.

● **Context clues** are specific clues in the sentences that can help you identify the meaning of the unfamiliar word.

> **Context Clues Text Marks**
>
> ⬭ Circle the **unfamiliar word**.
>
> ⎯ Underline **context clues**.
>
> ✎ Write the **meaning** of the unfamiliar word on the lines.

Read "A Precious Metal." Use context clues to figure out the meaning of an unfamiliar word and mark the text.

A Precious Metal

Gold is one of Earth's most valuable metals. Why is gold worth so much? First of all, it is one of the most **rare** metals. There is very little gold on Earth. On average, there are only 10 pounds of gold for every 2 billion pounds of dirt. Secondly, gold is very hard to find. Most gold lies hidden deep under the Earth. Miners have to dig it out and process it. To get 1 ounce of gold, it takes 100,000 ounces of ore!

> **Mark the Text**
>
> Use context clues to figure out the meaning of the word *rare*.
>
> ⬭ Circle the word *rare*.
>
> ⎯ Underline context clues.
>
> ✎ What is the meaning of *rare* in this passage?
>
> _____
>
> _____
>
> _____

Context Clues • Good as Gold • 2

Read "Hidden Treasure." Use context clues to figure out the meaning of unfamiliar words and mark the text.

Hidden Treasure

1   How do miners get gold out of the ground? They begin by drilling a large shaft into the earth. They put an elevator into the shaft to carry miners up and down. Miners dig out tunnels from the shaft under each **seam** of gold. Then they drill smaller tunnels up into the gold seams. Next, the miners put dynamite in the seams, leave the area, and set off the dynamite. The gold ore falls into trucks set up on rails.

2   The ore is **transported** in the trucks through the tunnels. Then it goes up the shaft to the surface of the mine. The ore is taken away to be processed. Finally, the gold is cast into bars. The bars are sent to special places where they are kept under lock and key!

Mark the Text

1   Use context clues to figure out the meaning of the word *seam*.

◯   Circle the word *seam*.

—   Underline context clues.

✎   What is the meaning of *seam* in this passage?

_____

_____

_____

2   Use context clues to figure out the meaning of the word *transported*.

◯   Circle the word *transported*.

—   Underline context clues.

✎   What is the meaning of *transported* in this passage?

_____

_____

_____

Text-Marking Lessons for Active Nonfiction Reading Grades 4–8 © 2012 by Judith Bauer Stamper, Scholastic Teaching Resources

Context Clues • Good as Gold • 3

Read "Panning for Gold." Use context clues to figure out the meaning of unfamiliar words and mark the text.

Panning for Gold

1   Not all gold is hidden under the earth. Gold also lies above ground. When **prospectors** pan for gold, they search at the bottom of riverbeds. They use a shovel to dig up dirt from the bottom of the stream. They use a pan to separate gold from the rocks and dirt.

2   How can you pan for a **nugget** of gold? To find a lump of the shiny metal, first, fill your pan with dirt from the river. Then, hold the pan just under the surface of the water. Shake it from side to side. Next, swirl the pan in circles. Heavier things, like a nugget of gold, sink to the bottom. Lighter things come to the top. Tilt the pan in the water and let the lighter material wash away. Then, check the bottom of your pan. With luck, you'll see a gold nugget shining there.

Mark the Text

1   Use context clues to figure out the meaning of the word *prospectors*.

⬭   Circle the word *prospectors*.

—   Underline context clues.

✎   What is the meaning of *prospectors* in this passage?

_____

_____

_____

2   Use context clues to figure out the meaning of the word *nugget*.

⬭   Circle the word *nugget*.

—   Underline context clues.

✎   What is the meaning of *nugget* in this passage?

_____

_____

_____

Text-Marking Lessons for Active Nonfiction Reading Grades 4–8 © 2012 by Judith Bauer Stamper, Scholastic Teaching Resources

Author's Purpose • Natural Wonders

1. Introduce the Skill

Ask students what they know about natural wonders in the United States. Prompt a discussion with these questions: *What do you know about the Grand Canyon? What might you see on a trip through the Everglades?* As they read about natural wonders, students should identify:

- The **author's purpose,** or the reason why the author is writing something.

- **Text evidence** that reveals the author's purpose.

- Whether the author's purpose is to **inform,** to **persuade,** or to **entertain.**

Continue following the Teaching Routine (pages 8–9) and use the lesson-specific tips for each remaining step.

2. Model

Model for students how to find the author's purpose in "The Grandest Canyon."

- *To find the author's purpose, I'll ask questions about why the author wrote this text. Then I'll look for text clues that can answer my questions.*

- *Is the author trying to persuade me, or convince me of something? No, I don't see language that is full of opinions or trying to persuade me.*

- *Is the author trying to entertain me? No, the language is serious and formal.*

- *Is the author trying to inform me about something? Yes, the text is full of facts about the Grand Canyon. I'll check the box "to inform" and underline sentences that give information.*

Materials

- Reading 1: "The Grandest Canyon"
  - page 55

- Reading 2: "Wild Water Rafting"/"My Mule Pokey" • page 56

- Reading 3: "Grassy Waters"/"Everglades Adventure" • page 57

3. Practice

Guide students to identify the author's purpose in "Wild Water Rafting" and "My Mule Pokey" by asking the following questions.

PARAGRAPH 1:

- *Is the author's purpose in "Wild Water Rafting" to inform, to persuade, or to entertain?*

- *What text evidence shows that the author's purpose is to persuade?*

PARAGRAPH 2:

- *What is the author's purpose in "My Mule Pokey"?*

- *What text evidence shows that the author's purpose is to entertain?*

4. Apply

Have students complete Reading 3 independently and then share their answers with partners or the group. Conclude by asking: *If you could choose between a trip to the Grand Canyon or the Everglades, which would you choose? Explain why.*

Text-Marking Lessons for Active Nonfiction Reading Grades 4–8 © 2012 by Judith Bauer Stamper, Scholastic Teaching Resources

Author's Purpose • Natural Wonders • 1

To help you figure out the author's purpose as you read, remember:

- The **author's purpose** is the reason why the author is writing something.

- The author's purpose can be to **inform**, to **persuade**, or to **entertain**.

- **Text clues** are words or sentences that reveal the author's purpose.

Author's Purpose Text Marks

✓ Check the author's **purpose:**
- ☐ to inform
- ☐ to persuade
- ☐ to entertain

⌣ Underline **text clues**.

Read "The Grandest Canyon." Identify the author's purpose and mark the text.

The Grandest Canyon

The Grand Canyon is a deep gorge that is 277 miles long and up to 18 miles wide. The Colorado River cut the canyon out of the surrounding rock. It took 3–6 million years to form. The Canyon is famous for the colored stripes of rock on its sides. Over 5 million people visit the Grand Canyon each year. They explore it on foot, on mules, and by raft on the Colorado River.

Mark the Text

Identify the author's purpose.

✓ Check the author's purpose:
- ☐ to inform
- ☐ to persuade
- ☐ to entertain

⌣ Underline three examples of text clues for the purpose.

Author's Purpose • Natural Wonders • 2

Read "Wild Water Rafting" and "My Mule Pokey." Identify the author's purpose for each reading. Then mark the text.

Wild Water Rafting

1 Do you want the trip of a lifetime? The staff at Canyon River Runners is ready to provide it. Our rafting trips through the Grand Canyon are wild and wonderful. Take a white-water raft ride on the Colorado River for three days. See the Grand Canyon from the bottom looking up. It's a wild ride that you'll never forget!

My Mule Pokey

2 Our guide introduced me to the mule I'd ride on down into the Grand Canyon. "This is Pokey," he said. I groaned with embarrassment. My brother started to laugh at me. Pokey looked at me and blinked his eyes. I let the guide boost me up onto Pokey's back. "Whoa!" I yelled as Pokey took off for the canyon rim. We stopped just short of the edge. I looked down for a mile into the bottom of the canyon.

"Take it a bit slower, Pokey," I said, patting my mule.

Mark the Text

1 Identify the author's purpose.

✓ Check the author's purpose:

☐ to inform

☐ to persuade

☐ to entertain

— Underline two text clues for the purpose.

2 Identify the author's purpose.

✓ Check the author's purpose:

☐ to inform

☐ to persuade

☐ to entertain

— Underline two text clues for the purpose.

Text-Marking Lessons for Active Nonfiction Reading Grades 4–8 © 2012 by Judith Bauer Stamper, Scholastic Teaching Resources

Author's Purpose • Natural Wonders • 3

Read "Grassy Waters" and "Everglades Adventure." Identify the author's purpose for each reading. Then mark the text.

Grassy Waters

1   The Everglades stretches across 1.5 million acres of grassy land. The land is often flooded by water. Ten thousand different islands make up the park. Many different types of animals live in the Everglades. What animal do visitors want to see most? Everyone hopes to see an alligator snapping its big jaws.

Everglades Adventure

2   I paddled my kayak through the winding waterways of the Everglades. My dad was in front of me. No one was behind me, unless an alligator was there. What if it was watching and waiting? Suddenly, I heard a loud plop in the water beside me. I screamed. A big alligator's head rose up beside my kayak. The gator opened its jaws and seemed to laugh at me. Then it sunk slowly back under the water.

Mark the Text

1 Identify the author's purpose.

✓ Check the author's purpose:

☐ to inform

☐ to persuade

☐ to entertain

— Underline two text clues for the purpose.

2 Identify the author's purpose.

✓ Check the author's purpose:

☐ to inform

☐ to persuade

☐ to entertain

— Underline two text clues for the purpose.

Text-Marking Lessons for Active Nonfiction Reading Grades 4–8 © 2012 by Judith Bauer Stamper, Scholastic Teaching Resources

Answer Key

‖‖‖

LESSON 1 PAGE 11

Fifty Nifty Names

State names come from many places, just like the American people. The Native Americans named many places in North America. That's why 27 state names come from Native American words. What about the other states? Some have the names of kings and queens in Europe. Some have names from other languages. Only one state has the name of an American president. Can you guess which one?

LESSON 1 PAGE 12

Native Names

1 Over half our states have Native American names. Iowa and Missouri are both named after their rivers. How were the rivers named? The Iowa River takes its name from the *Ayuwha* or *Iowa* tribe. The Missouri River is named for the Missouri people. Their name means "people with the dugout canoes."

2 Connecticut is named after a Mohegan Indian word. It means "beside the long tidal river." Mississippi's name comes from several sources. The Algonquin Indians called the river "messipi." The Chippewa called it "mici zibi." All the languages agree on one thing. It is a great river. European settlers made up the name for Indiana. It means "Land of the Indians."

LESSON 1 PAGE 13

Kings and Colors

1 Explorers and settlers from Europe named about half the states. Several states have royal names. English settlers named Georgia after King George II. A French explorer named Louisiana after King Louis XIV of France. Four states start with "New." New Hampshire, New Jersey, and New York have English names. New Mexico takes its name from its neighbor, Mexico.

2 Several states have colorful names. Colorado means "reddish color" in Spanish. Spanish explorers named it for its reddish rocks. French explorers named Vermont. They loved its tree-covered "green mountains." What state is named after an American president? That's right—Washington!

LESSON 2 PAGE 15

Buzz and Bite

People all over the world are scratching their mosquito bites. Why do mosquitoes like to bite? A female mosquito needs blood to make more mosquitoes. The female's mouth has a special part. She uses it to suck blood. She shoots some of her saliva into a person. It makes the blood easier to drink. The mosquito's saliva is what makes a bite itch. Yuk!

LESSON 2 PAGE 16

That Stings!

1 Don't make a bee or wasp mad at you. Bees and wasps fight back with their stingers when they are disturbed or angry. A honeybee can sting a person only once. Its stinger gets stuck inside the victim's body. The honeybee dies after just one sting. Wasps, like hornets and yellow jackets, can pull their stingers out. So, they can sting their victims over and over again.

2 A bee or wasp sting hurts when it happens, and it keeps on hurting. After a sting, the skin becomes hot, turns red, and starts to itch. It's always best to remove the stinger as soon as possible. Some people are very allergic to insect stings. They might get hives, become dizzy, and have problems breathing. A little insect sting can cause big trouble.

LESSON 2 PAGE 17

Bad Bug Bites

1 Two spiders that live in the United States have poisonous bites. They are the black widow and the brown recluse spiders. A black widow spider has a black, shiny body with a red-orange or yellow mark on its stomach. The brown recluse spider is brown with long, skinny legs. If these spiders bite you, the bite will swell, hurt, and make you feel really sick. Few people die from the spider bites. But if one of these spiders bite you, it's important to see a doctor right away.

2 A deer tick is a tiny insect that can cause a bad disease. The tick attaches its six legs to the skin of a victim and sucks its blood. Humans can get Lyme disease, a hard-to-cure illness, from the bacteria in the tick's bite. If you find a tick on your skin, pull it off with a tweezer. Then take the tick to your doctor to be checked.

Tsunami Survivor

On [December 26, 2004,]¹ an earthquake under the Indian Ocean caused a terrifying tsunami. Ari Afrizal was building a house when a 30-foot high wall of water crashed over him. [Soon after,]² he was swept out to sea. [For an hour,]³ he managed to stay afloat. [Then]⁴ he grabbed hold of a wooden plank. [The next day,]⁵ he climbed aboard a leaky fishing boat. On the boat, Ari ate coconuts that floated by and watched shark fins circle around him. [Finally,]⁶ Ari was rescued by a passing ship. He had survived for an amazing 15 da___

Air Crash Survivor

In [December, 1971,]¹ Juliane Koepcke boarded a plane. She was headed for the Amazon rainforest to visit her father. [An hour later]² a bolt of lightning hit the plane. [Then]³ it exploded into pieces in midair. [Next]⁴ Juliane found herself spinning through the air. She fell more than two miles before landing in the thick jungle. [For the next ten days]⁵ Juliane walked through the dangerous rainforest. She followed creeks and rivers. She waded through water filled with crocodiles. [At last]⁶ she found a hut and was rescued. [Later]⁷ Juliane learned that she was the only survivor of the crash.

Earthquake Survivor

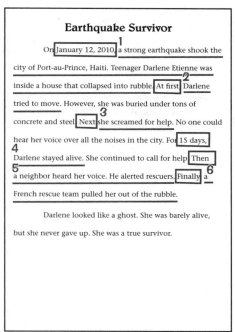

On [January 12, 2010,]¹ a strong earthquake shook the city of Port-au-Prince, Haiti. Teenager Darlene Etienne was inside a house that collapsed into rubble. [At first]² Darlene tried to move. However, she was buried under tons of concrete and steel. [Next]³ she screamed for help. No one could hear her voice over all the noises in the city. [For 15 days,]⁴ Darlene stayed alive. She continued to call for help. [Then]⁵ a neighbor heard her voice. He alerted rescuers. [Finally]⁶ a French rescue team pulled her out of the rubble.

Darlene looked like a ghost. She was barely alive, but she never gave up. She was a true survivor.

The Amazing Amazon

(The Amazon is the largest tropical rain forest in the world.) It covers about 40 percent of South America. Rain forests are in very warm parts of the earth. They also get a rainfall of at least 100 inches each year. Rain forests are home to a huge variety of living things. The Amazon has the most species of plants and animals of any place in the world.

The Amazon, in South America, is the world's largest rain forest. It is warm, rainy, and full of many different plants and animals.

Amazon Journey

Many people want to protect the Amazon rain forest. But few care as much as Ed Stafford. (Stafford is the first person to ever hike the entire length of the Amazon River.) Stafford started at the river's source in Peru. He ended where the river flows into the ocean in Brazil. The journey stretched for 4,200 miles through the rain forest.

Along the way, Stafford waded through dangerous waters. They were full of hungry piranha fish and crocodiles. On land, he met snakes, jaguars, and millions of mosquitoes. Almost two and a half years later, Stafford finished his hike. He did it to call the world's attention to saving the Amazon.

Ed Stafford is the first person to hike the entire Amazon River. He hiked 4,200 miles in 2 1/2 years.

A Rain Forest in Trouble

(Even though it is a huge place, the Amazon is in trouble.) In just a few decades, the Amazon has lost almost 17 percent of its trees. Experts worry what will happen next. They predict that 55 percent of the Amazon might be destroyed by 2030.

Humans are destroying the Amazon for their own use. Farmers clear land to raise cattle and crops. Loggers cut down trees to make cheap timber. Roads, mines, and gas lines all add to the problem.

Other people are working hard to save the Amazon. Rain forests are the source of many foods and medicines. Rain forests absorb carbon dioxide, release oxygen, and keep the planet healthy. Saving the Amazon means saving the planet.

Humans are destroying the Amazon by cutting down trees. Some people want to protect the Amazon and its resources. Saving the Amazon is saving the planet.

Answer Key

LESSON 5 PAGE 27

Mount St. Helens Blows Up!

Mount St. Helens is a volcano in the state of Washington. For many years, it was inactive. Then, in 1980, it started to show signs of life. On May 18, the volcano blew up. A violent eruption caused the mountain to explode and shoot out lava, rocks, ash, and gas. As a result of the eruption, 57 people died and countless animals and plants were destroyed. It was the deadliest eruption ever in the United States.

LESSON 5 PAGE 28

When Volcanoes Explode

1 When a volcano explodes, it destroys everything around it. Lava—red hot, melted rock—spurts out of the top. Because the lava is so hot and thick it burns everything in its path. That includes trees, houses, and even cars. The lava turns into hard rock when it cools.

2 An erupting volcano also shoots out huge clouds of ash mixed with poisonous gases. Sometimes the clouds of ash are so thick and high that they block out the sun. As a result, the climate of the area can grow cooler. Thick ash clouds are also a danger to jet planes. The ash can make a plane crash by clogging up its engines.

If you are ever near an erupting volcano, don't waste time. Run for your life!

LESSON 5 PAGE 29

Ash From Iceland

1 In the spring of 2010, a volcano in Iceland made world headlines. The volcano's name is Eyjafjallajökull. It sits under a large ice cap near the Arctic Circle. The volcano began to erupt in late March. Its fiery heat melted the ice above it, causing rivers to flood and forcing residents to evacuate.

2 Things really started to heat up on April 14. The volcano shot up clouds containing millions of fine pieces of glassy ash. The ash drifted high into the air over Europe. As a result, governments would not allow planes to take off or land. Millions of travelers were stranded in airports. Almost a week passed before the airports opened again. A small volcano showed the world the power of nature.

LESSON 6 PAGE 31

Wilma Rudolph

People called her "the fastest woman in history." In 1960, Wilma Rudolph won three gold medals at a single Olympics. It was a great achievement for any athlete. For Rudolph, it was amazing. She had polio as a child. The disease left her left leg paralyzed. With the help of doctors, Rudolph walked again by age 12. Only eight years later, she went to the Olympics and ran off with the gold.

Wilma Rudolph must have been a very determined, hard-working person.

LESSON 6 PAGE 32

Bruce Lee

1 Bruce Lee was weak and sickly as a child. As a teenager, he had to protect himself in his tough neighborhood. So, he took up martial arts. Lee studied every kind of physical fighting. He worked out constantly. He did sit-ups while watching TV. He practiced kicks while walking down the street. He quickly became a master of the martial arts.

He became an expert quickly because he spent all his time practicing martial arts.

2 Bruce Lee made martial arts popular in the United States. He amazed audiences with his karate and kung fu skills. He wrote and directed martial arts movies and starred in them himself. He became the highest paid actor in the world, as well as an amazing athlete. Because of Bruce Lee, millions of U.S. kids became fans of the martial arts.

He had a lot of talents and had the confidence and drive to succeed.

LESSON 6 PAGE 33

Pele

1 Who is the most famous soccer star of all time? Most people will answer with just one name—Pele. Pele grew up in Brazil. He kicked a grapefruit around as his first soccer ball. Next he practiced with an old sock stuffed with newspapers. Then he started to play with a real soccer ball in school. People knew right away that he was a star.

Pele must have been poor as a child because he didn't have a soccer ball to play with.

2 At seventeen, Pele's amazing talent put him on Brazil's World Cup team. He scored the only goals in Brazil's World Cup victory. One goal was his famous "bicycle" kick backwards. Years later, Brazilians watched as Pele kicked his one thousandth goal. The crowd cheered their hero for eleven minutes!

Fans in Brazil must have loved Pele for winning the World Cup and for his amazing soccer talent.

Buried Alive!

An earthquake sends shock waves through the ground. Buildings fall down into piles of rubble. Rescuing people buried under the rubble is a huge challenge. Rescue teams have special ways to solve the problem. They use microphones to hear the victims. They use dogs to locate them. Then they tunnel through the rubble to pull out the survivors.

Air Lifts

1 In an avalanche, snow comes crashing down a mountain. People in the way face a terrible problem. They are buried under a ton of snow. How do they survive? Mountain rescue teams solve the problem. They fly helicopters into the area. They find survivors by radio signals or rescue dogs. Then they dig out the victims. Sometimes, there are just minutes to spare.

2 Heavy rains cause flash floods. With little warning, people are trapped in their houses by floodwaters. There is no way to walk, drive, or swim away. Helicopters solve the problem by flying into flood areas. Rescuers lift people off their roofs and carry them to safety.

Animal Emergencies

1 Even animals need special rescues. Every year, a number of whales lose their way in the ocean. They become stranded on beaches. It's a big problem to get them back into the water. Rescue teams fix the problem with a crane. They lift up the whale in a big canvas sling. Then they drop it back into the ocean.

2 Oil slicks are a deadly problem for coastal birds. When oil coats the birds' feathers, they can't fly or clean themselves. Rescuers solve the problem by cleaning the feathers with a special chemical. Then they return the birds to their homes in nature.

Komodo Dragons

The world of lizards is full of strange, scaly animals, but one lizard stands out from the rest. It is called the Komodo dragon. Like other lizards, Komodo dragons have scaly skin. They also lays eggs to have their young like other lizards. However, Komodo dragons are much bigger than other lizards. They can weigh up to three hundred pounds. The amount they eat is different as well. They can finish off several wild pigs for lunch.

Vampire Bats

1 Many people find bats a little creepy. One kind of bat is really creepy. It is called a vampire bat. Like other bats, the vampire bat is a mammal. A mammal is covered by hair or fur and gives birth to live babies. Vampire bats are also like other bats in where they live. They hang out in dark places like caves, and they sleep during the day and fly at night.

2 However, there are big differences between vampire bats and other bats. Most bats eat insects or small animals like mice. A vampire bat is different in what it eats. It feeds entirely on blood! Vampire bats bite livestock like cows and lap up their blood for half an hour. How can you recognize a vampire bat? Its teeth are different from those of other bats. They are longer and sharper. Creepy!

Great White Sharks

1 Do sharks deserve their bloodthirsty reputation? One shark—the great white shark—deserves all the respect it gets. Like all sharks, great white sharks have no bones. Instead of bones, shark skeletons are made of cartilage, which is like the end of a human nose. In addition, great whites and other sharks both have many rows of teeth that fall out and grow back easily.

2 The great white shark is different from other sharks in its size. It is the largest predator in the sea. It can grow up to 20 feet long and weigh up to 4,500 pounds. The great white is also different from other sharks in its feeding habits. It is the most vicious hunter. It often attacks its prey from below, ripping it apart in its huge jaws. If you see the fin of a great white shark, it's time to get out of the water!

Answer Key

LESSON 9 PAGE 43

Champion Skippers

The Summerville Skippers are a jump rope group from Boise, Idaho. They won the World Championship Title for Team USA. That title is equal to the Olympics of Jump Rope. In 2010, five Skippers competed in a Guinness World Records Day celebration. The three girls and two boys set a new record for Double-Dutch style skips. What was their record-breaking number? It was 371 skips in a row!

Double Dutch means that a team of jumpers jump rope at the same time.

LESSON 9 PAGE 44

Youngest Climber

In May 2010, 13-year-old Jordan Romero set a world record. Even more amazing, he did it on top of the world! Jordan climbed to the summit of Mount Everest. It is the highest mountain in the world. He became the youngest person ever to climb Everest.

Jordan made the climb with his father, his mother, and three Sherpas. Jordan hopes to climb the Seven Summits. Those are the highest points on all seven continents. Reactions to Jordan's climb were mixed. Many people think he is a hero. Others think a 13-year-old shouldn't be on Everest. Every year, climbers die on the mountain. One thing is for sure, Jordan is a top teen athlete.

Climbing Everest is so dangerous that people die trying each year. A teenager like Jordan is too young to risk his life.

LESSON 9 PAGE 45

Wheelchair Champ

Aaron Fotheringham is a true champ. He was born with spina bifida. The disease paralyzed him from the waist down. But getting around in a wheelchair hasn't stopped Aaron. When he was just 8, he went to a skateboard park. Ten years later, he is a record-setter on his wheelchair skateboard.

In 2008, Aaron landed a single back flip in his wheelchair. Right away, Aaron set a new goal for himself. He would try a double back flip. Aaron attempted the trick over and over again. Finally, in 2010, Aaron did it. He flew off a ramp, landed a double back flip, and went into the record books.

What does a champ do next? Aaron is working with disabled children. He hopes to inspire them to reach their own dreams.

Aaron is a champ because he keeps trying to excel at his sport. He doesn't let his paralyzed legs stop him.

LESSON 10 PAGE 47

Should Students Go to School Year-Round?

In Germany and Japan, students go to school year-round. In the United States, students have two or more month's vacation. Should American students to be in class 12 months a year?

Some experts believe that summer vacation hurts education. They say students forget what they have learned. However, many parents think that kids need a break from school. Who do you think is right?

LESSON 10 PAGE 48

Should Girls Play On Boys' Sports Teams?

In 1972, Congress passed a law called Title IX. It states that girls and boys should have equal opportunities in school. The law changed school sports forever. The number of girls playing high school sports grew from 30,000 in 1972 to over 170,000 today. Many girls now want to play on boys' sports teams.

Some people think that a girl playing on a boys' team is wrong. They say girls are weaker and could get hurt. They argue that it's not fair to the boys on the teams. Other people believe that girls have as much right to play as boys. If a girl is good enough to make a team, she should be able to play on it. There are strong opinions on both sides of the issue.

LESSON 10 PAGE 49

Should Cell Phones Be Allowed in School?

A recent survey shows that 75 percent of teens between ages 12 and 17 have their own cell phones. They carry them everywhere, including to school. That has caused a big debate. Kids use their cell phones to talk, to text, and to take pictures. However, problems come up when kids have cell phones in schools. Over two-thirds of high schools have banned cell phones.

Many teachers believe that cell phones interfere with learning. Kids might check their phones for text messages. A call can disrupt a class. Many parents feel their kids should carry cell phones. They like being able to get in touch with their kids. They think the phones keep their kids safe.

What do you think? Should kids have cell phones in school?

A Precious Metal

Gold is one of Earth's most valuable metals. Why is gold worth so much? First of all, it is one of the most **rare** metals. There is very little gold on Earth. On average, there are only 10 pounds of gold for every 2 billion pounds of dirt. Secondly, gold is very hard to find. Most gold lies hidden deep under the Earth. Miners have to dig it out and process it. To get 1 ounce of gold, it takes 100,000 ounces of ore!

Rare means uncommon or unusual.

Hidden Treasure

1 How do miners get gold out of the ground? They begin by drilling a large shaft into the earth. They put an elevator into the shaft to carry miners up and down. Miners dig out tunnels from the shaft under each **seam** of gold. Then they drill smaller tunnels up into the gold seams. Next, the miners put dynamite in the seams, leave the area, and set off the dynamite. The gold ore falls into trucks set up on rails.

2 The ore is **transported** in the trucks through the tunnels. Then it goes up the shaft to the surface of the mine. The ore is taken away to be processed. Finally, the gold is cast into bars. The bars are sent to special places where they are kept under lock and key!

1. Seam means a layer of something like gold.

2. Transported means moved or carried.

Panning for Gold

1 Not all gold is hidden under the earth. Gold also lies above ground. When **prospectors** pan for gold, they search at the bottom of riverbeds. They use a shovel to dig up dirt from the bottom of the stream. They use a pan to separate gold from the rocks and dirt.

2 How can you pan for a **nugget** of gold? To find a lump of the shiny metal, first, fill your pan with dirt from the river. Then, hold the pan just under the surface of the water. Shake it from side to side. Next, swirl the pan in circles. Heavier things, like a nugget of gold, sink to the bottom. Lighter things come to the top. Tilt the pan in the water and let the lighter material wash away. Then, check the bottom of your pan. With luck, you'll see a gold nugget shining there.

1. A prospector is a person who explores an area for gold.

2. A nugget is a solid lump of precious metal.

The Grandest Canyon

The Grand Canyon is a deep gorge that is 277 miles long and up to 18 miles wide. The Colorado River cut the canyon out of the surrounding rock. It took 3–6 million years to form. The Canyon is famous for the colored stripes of rock on its sides. Over 5 million people visit the Grand Canyon each year. They explore it on foot, on mules, and by raft on the Colorado River.

 to inform

Wild Water Rafting

1 Do you want the trip of a lifetime? The staff at Canyon River Runners is ready to provide it. Our rafting trips through the Grand Canyon are wild and wonderful. Take a white-water raft ride on the Colorado River for three days. See the Grand Canyon from the bottom looking up. It's a wild ride that you'll never forget!

☑ to persuade

My Mule Pokey

2 Our guide introduced me to the mule I'd ride on down into the Grand Canyon. "This is Pokey," he said. I groaned with embarrassment. My brother started to laugh at me. Pokey looked at me and blinked his eyes. I let the guide boost me up onto Pokey's back. "Whoa!" I yelled as Pokey took off for the canyon rim. We stopped just short of the edge. I looked down for a mile into the bottom of the canyon.

"Take it a bit slower, Pokey," I said, patting my mule.

☑ to entertain

Grassy Waters

1 The Everglades stretches across 1.5 million acres of grassy land. The land is often flooded by water. Ten thousand different islands make up the park. Many different types of animals live in the Everglades. What animal do visitors want to see most? Everyone hopes to see an alligator snapping its big jaws.

☑ to inform

Everglades Adventure

2 I paddled my kayak through the winding waterways of the Everglades. My dad was in front of me. No one was behind me, unless an alligator was there. What if it was watching and waiting? Suddenly, I heard a loud plop in the water beside me. I screamed. A big alligator's head rose up beside my kayak. The gator opened its jaws and seemed to laugh at me. Then it sunk slowly back under the water.

 to entertain

Lesson-by-Lesson Connections to the Common Core State Standards

LESSON	READING STANDARDS FOR INFORMATIONAL TEXT
1	RI.4.1: Refer to details and examples in a text when explaining what the text says explicitly. RI.5.1: Quote accurately from a text when explaining what the text says explicitly. RI.6.1: Cite textual evidence to support analysis of what the text says explicitly. RI.7.1: Cite several pieces of textual evidence to support analysis of what the text says explicitly. RI.8.1: Cite the textual evidence that most strongly supports an analysis of what the text says explicitly.
2	RI.4.2: Determine the main idea of a text and explain how it is supported by key details. RI.5.2: Determine two or more main ideas of a text and explain how they are supported by key details. RI.6.2: Determine a central idea of a text and how it is conveyed through particular details. RI.7.2: Determine two or more central ideas in a text and analyze their development over the course of the text. RI.8.2: Determine a central idea of a text and analyze its development over the course of the text, including its relationship to supporting ideas.
3	RI.4.5: Describe the overall structure (e.g., chronology) of events, ideas, concepts, or information in a text or part of a text. RI.5.3: Explain the relationships or interactions between two or more individuals, events, ideas, or concepts in a historical, scientific, or technical text based on specific information in the text. RI.5.5: Compare and contrast the overall structure (e.g., chronology) of events, ideas, concepts, or information in two or more texts. RI.6.5: Analyze how a particular sentence, paragraph, chapter, or section fits into the overall structure of a text and contributes to the development of the ideas. RI.7.5: Analyze the structure an author uses to organize a text, including how the major sections contribute to the whole and to the development of the ideas. RI.8.5: Analyze in detail the structure of a specific paragraph in a text, including the role of particular sentences in developing and refining a key concept.
4	RI.4.2: Determine the main idea of a text and explain how it is supported by key details; summarize the text. RI.5.2: Determine two or more main ideas of a text and explain how they are supported by key details; summarize the text. RI.6.2: Determine a central idea of a text and how it is conveyed through particular details; provide a summary of the text distinct from personal opinions or judgments. RI.7.2: Determine two or more central ideas in a text and analyze their development over the course of the text; provide an objective summary of the text. RI.8.2: Determine a central idea of a text and analyze its development over the course of the text, including its relationship to supporting ideas; provide an objective summary of the text.
5	RI.4.3: Explain events, procedures, ideas, or concepts in a historical, scientific, or technical text, including what happened and why, based on specific information in the text. RI.4.5: Describe the overall structure (e.g., chronology, comparison, cause/effect, problem/solution) of events, ideas, concepts, or information in a text or part of a text. RI.5.3: Explain the relationships or interactions between two or more individuals, events, ideas, or concepts in a historical, scientific, or technical text based on specific information in the text. RI.5.5: Compare and contrast the overall structure (e.g., chronology, comparison, cause/effect, problem/solution) of events, ideas, concepts, or information in two or more texts. RI.6.3: Analyze in detail how a key individual, event, or idea is introduced, illustrated, and elaborated in a text (e.g., through examples or anecdotes). RI.6.5: Analyze how a particular sentence, paragraph, chapter, or section fits into the overall structure of a text and contributes to the development of the ideas. RI.7.3: Analyze the interactions between individuals, events, and ideas in a text (e.g., how ideas influence individuals or events, or how individuals influence ideas or events). RI.7.5: Analyze the structure an author uses to organize a text, including how the major sections contribute to the whole and to the development of the ideas. RI.8.3: Analyze how a text makes connections among and distinctions between individuals, ideas, or events (e.g., through comparisons, analogies, or categories). RI.8.5: Analyze in detail the structure of a specific paragraph in a text, including the role of particular sentences in developing and refining a key concept.